Vagrant Verses by Rosa Mulholland

Rosa Mulholland was born at some point in 1841, an exact date is not known, in Belfast, Ireland.

At first her chosen career was to be a painter but by the age of 15 she had turned to a literary life and attempted to publish her first book.

She did submit several comical illustrations to Punch, but they were declined. However, Charles Dickens did review her work and encouraged her to continue writing.

Having spent some years in the rugged west of Ireland, Rosa used the landscape and characters to help fuel her writing talents.

Her twenty-two stanza poem 'Irene' (1862) was published by The Cornhill Magazine under her pseudonym 'Ruth Murray' with illustrations by the Pre-Raphaelite painter John Everett Millais.

Her first novel published was 'Dunmara' (1864), was also written as by 'Ruth Murray'. This story of an Irish girl raised in Spain who makes her way in London as an artist, somewhat reflecting her own aspirations. Despite the rise of Female activism Mulholland supported but did not offer overt support in her writing, tending to present her heroines as 'good wives.' She noticed how women struggled for happiness in a world where erotic love and marriage were tied to issues of material security.

Charles Dickens had published her in 'All the Year Round'. He even went as so far to suggest that her two novels, 'Hester's History' (1869) and 'The Wicked Woods of Tobereevil' (1872) be written for his periodical, then edited by himself. Dickens also republished two short stories 'The Late Miss Hollingford' (1886) and 'Eldergowan' (1874).

Rosa's poetry was almost always well received by both critics and the public ever since 'Irene' had been published. The poems were released collectively as the 'Vagrant Verses', in 1886.

Her novel of 1886, 'Marcella Gray', was first serialized in The Irish Monthly, and offered the example of a beneficent Catholic landowner as a solution to the Irish Question.

On 29th May 1891 Rosa, by now also a devout Catholic, married John Thomas Gilbert, a renowned Dublin historian at St. Mary's Pro Cathedral in Dublin. Gilbert's history books were very valued and he was knighted in 1897, Rosa then assumed the title of Lady Gilbert.

In her later years, she wrote fiction with strong-minded, independent women as heroines, and were directed mainly at young readers. These included 'Banshee Castle' (1895), 'The Walking Trees & Other Tales (1897), 'Spirit and Dust' (1908) and 'Dreams and Realities' (1916), Rosa also wrote a biography of her husband in 1905, who had died abruptly in 1898. She recounted that after a pleasant morning spent by the couple in their villa, Sir Gilbert had left alone to attend a meeting of the Council of the Royal Irish Academy, and died of sudden heart failure en-route.

Rosa Mulholland, Lady Gilbert, died in Dublin, Ireland in on 21st April 1921 and is buried in Glasnevin Cemetery.

Index of Contents

VAGRANT VERSES

EMMET'S LOVE

In yon green garden, sweet with hawthorn-breath,
Knee-deep in flowers we talked of love and faith,
O year-dead Love, and, smiling, you and I,
We did not think of death.

The crimson rose, with rain-drops 'neath its hood,
I plucked for you reeked not with tears of blood.
Like these I gather now; we did not sigh
When past us from the wood

The night owl whirred, as silver-sandalled Eve,
With floating veils around her, 'gan to weave
Sad spells across the grass, and at our ears
Made the young pigeons grieve.

We had no sorrow; all that life we knew
Was like our summer walk 'neath skies as blue
As violet-drifts, and we could see our years
Before us in the dew,

Like miles of hawthorn bloom the lanes along,
That slant toward purple rain-mists out among
The sunlit hills, while all the perfumed air
Is sweet with thrushes' song.

I had no fear save that some nobler eyes
Might win my love from me, so little wise,
So weak and small, although you called me fair
With love that glorifies.

And I was jealous once. 'Twas thus it came:
I heard you say some other woman's name
I knew not, and my wits were all undone,
My heart was in a flame,

Till out you laughed, such laughter good, and cried,
"The land, my love! Are you or she my bride?
No other rival have you but this one,
Erin, the queen sad-eyed!"

And then you told me, for I had not known,
Pent in this garden, how the land made moan,
The lovely flower-faced land that gave us life,
A queen without a throne —

A beggar queen, with bare feet in the snows.
No crown upon her head, and no sweet rose
Within her breast, with soft hands scarred from strife,
Who weepeth as she goes,

A vagrant 'mid the kings and queens of time,
Yet ever lovely in the gracious prime
Of beauty nourished by her children's love;
Though monarchs fall and climb,

Still lives she 'mid the bramble and the thorn,
Her fair face lifted to eternal morn,
While nest with her the lark and the pale dove
In the shamrock grass unshorn.

Weeping I heard, and cried your heart, I knew.
Was Erin's more than mine. Love, it was true.
For her you died, and where so cold you lie,

Under the shamrock dew,

I am forgot, and she is mourning still.
But then you chid me, telling many an ill
Her children bore, like savage beasts at bay
In hunted wood and hill.

While all the thick-draped, wide-armed, friendly trees
That hid their woes were fired against the breeze.
And near the mounds of flame the slave-ship lay
Fast-bound for foreign seas:

How in the mountain cave the priest was snared,
The law-breaker who death and torture dared
With Christ's red wine-cup in his obstinate hand,
And crucifix all bared:

How you yourself, beneath the sick moon's beam,
Had heard strange flutterings and an eagle's scream,
And seen, a rood across the haunted land,
As in a horrid dream.

The dead Franciscan, in his monkish gown,
His cord of poverty and shaven-crown.
Swing from the bough, and with the irreverent winds.
Go wavering up and down.

I had not known, here in this garden green.
Walled high with poplars and the tall beech screen
Of hedges, where the white the red rose binds,
Such things had ever been.

My days had been so fair, so tranquil sweet.
Until you came and made the world's heart beat
For me, and 'twixt the fluttering of the flowers
Showed me the yellowing wheat.

Love's harvest growing, our life's sustenance.
Out in the open where the shadows dance.
Dropped from the hill-tops with the slanting showers,
Down-driven by many a lance,

And glittering spear of sunshine. Our birthright
That field of golden grain and waving light.
And flame of poppies cooled with steadfast blue
Of meeker blossoms bright.

I had not known, nor yet full knowledge came

Until your sudden sword leaped out in flame
Of hate for tyranny, and struck the Untrue
That willed your death of shame,

On that red day that drained my world of tears:
A dry old world, unknowing hopes or fears,
That weeps no more, but only groans and turns
The wheel of its slow years;

Asking for you with eyes that strain, and stare,
And will not close though seeing you nowhere,
While every floweret for a rain-drop burns
Under a mad sun's glare;

Save when the tender night will sometimes have
A drop of dew for your unhonoured grave.
In that green gloom unnamed where she, your queen,
Hides all her vanquished brave,

Erin, the queen who won you. She hath yet
Full many a love will woo her to forget.
She lies not prone upon one spot of green.
Seeking with dews to wet.

With dews of grass to wet her withering eyes;
Sweet tears as ever 'neath her fair lids rise,
To float her smiles along the coming years
Toward new love's sympathies.

She might have left me you, O year-dead Love
It is not she who craves you from above,
And from below, with eyes that have no tears.
And voice like that wood dove

That ever moans, moans, moans and has no word
To tell her pain, — not Erin, whom your sword
Leaped for, — not she of whom you dreamed,
And with your death adored.

For her you died. Now would I that you might
Have turned on me your sword, and in the light
Have lived for her. Full sweet to me had seemed
Forgetfulness and night.

O we have strained through toil of years,
My heart, to reach one golden day,
And looked for it through blinding tears
Across the salt sea spray!
Say, say.
Will it be yea or nay,
My heart?
Will ever its fair sun rise for us, our flower-faced,
sweet-breath'd day?

O we have seen it dawn flame-red,
My heart, and lived our golden day, —
O cruel scent of roses shed
That haunts us now alway.
Say, say,
Wherefore it passed away,
My heart,
So swift, and left us in midnight, our life's one
summer-day?

A LULLABY

The sweet soft shadows of the summer night
Have stilled all fevered things that throb in light
To rest, my heart:
Lullaby, my heart, my heart!

The wind has ceased to sob in cave forlorn,
The moor-bird lies with bleeding breast and torn
At rest, my heart:
Lullaby, my heart, my heart!

At highest tide the passion of thy tears
Wears not the rock of fate: sleep through thy years,
And rest, my heart!
Lullaby, my heart, my heart!

Drink thy sweet draught of death, and wake no more
Till morning hail thee on a new day's shore;
Now rest, my heart!
Lullaby, my heart, my heart!

THITHER

In a little chamber above the sea
One lay dying, ah, well-a-day!
And the ocean prayeth unceasingly
When earth's young creatures are fading away!

The wild bird sang from the green, green wood,
Outpouring its joy in a lonely ear:
"O, love is lovely and life is good
In the glory and flush of the blooming year!"

The sweet blue rock-doves made their moan:
"Ah wherefore go, and ah wherefore go,
Alone, alone, to the world unknown,
From the dear green earth that hath loved you so?"

The roses unfolded one by one,
And happy creatures with lustrous eyes
Gazed through shadows into the sun
At the purple flash of the dragon-flies.

But the lonely, lamenting, chiming sea,
With its prayerful chant and its loud "Amen,"
Kept sighing its vespers dolefully.
As the tides beat in and beat out again.

And its tracks of light looked long and wide
To the lone sad soul that was sick to death;
"O Christ!" he cried, "O Christ, who died,
All nature bloometh and quickeneth,

"While I alone lie faint and prone.
With broken spirit and longing heart,
Too weak to travel to worlds unknown.
Seeking Thy shelter where'er Thou art!"

Down sank the sun, and the wood-doves slept,
Housed were all warm soft-breathing things.
The rose was hidden, and sweet dews wept,
The moon hung high on her silver wings;

All pale were the ocean's tracks of light.
When out of the gloom with a ghostly prow
A boat came glimmering over the night —
Oh, who is this with the radiant brow?

"Arise!" said the Lord, "and sail with me!"
And the faint sad soul came trembling forth
All fresh in the youth of eternity,

And they sailed not south, nor sailed they north,

But into the kingdom of endless bloom.
Do wood-doves call in its forests fair?
Do roses burn in a soft green gloom?
We dream and wonder, we follow not there.

SAINT BARBARA

O pure white Barbara, O cruel fate!
In a high and narrow tower
They have made for thy youth a strange and lonely bower,
So dread by night, and so forlorn by day:
From the warm world of love too far away,
Thou weep'st in lofty state!

Sadly thy gentle spirit hath obeyed
A father unforgiven
Who hid thy face among the clouds of heaven:
Yet with the lore and wisdom of the sages
Thy beauty shines to us across the ages,
A bloom Time cannot fade.

Girl, they have cut from 'neath thy dancing feet
Earth with her rose and lily,
Her violet and her light-winged daffodilly—
Stole from thine ear the sound of children singing;
The low of kine and pleasant sheep-bells ringing
Are silent to thee, sweet!

No tender human fingers touch thine own;
The cold winds round thy bed
Caress thy motherless young golden head.
The silence widens not when thou art sleeping,
Save by the absence of thy hopeless weeping,
Echoed by walls of stone.

Yet thou hast company the clouds among,
The birds' loud songs surround thee,
The legions of the storm whirl round and round thee;
The tranquil saints, from their eternal places.
Look out and show thee their enraptured faces —
The stars shine clear and long.

To such high company thy soul doth leap,
The lark's wild hymn repeating,

Flinging the tempest thine impassioned greeting,
Watching the stars until thine eyes become
A-fire amidst them in the midnight gloom,
No longer doomed to weep.

The rifts in heaven grow wider day by day.
And the tender eyes in glory
Look down in thine and tell thee a heavenly story;
The years go, and the light and darkness flitting,
They are not known to thee where thou art sitting
Dreaming thy life away.

A band of fair young angels comes to thee,
Down to thy narrow chamber,
With lutes in their hands and trailing wings of amber;
And I try to see thee there amid their splendour.
But my eyes fail me with a swift surrender
To daisies under me.

The daisies are for me, and the young grass,
And the birds in the low hedges.
Yet whenever I see the clouds with their golden edges
I think of thee in thy tower among the angels
Drinking the comfort of their pure evangels,
Sweetest of Barbaras!

LOVE AND DEATH

In the wild autumn weather, when the rain was on the sea,
And the boughs sobbed together. Death came and spake to me;
"Those red drops of thy heart I have come to take from thee;
As the storm sheds the rose, so thy love shall broken be,"
     Said Death to me.

Then I stood straight and fearless while the rain was in the wave,
And I spake low and tearless: " When thou hast made my grave,
Those red drops from my heart then thou shalt surely have;
But the rose keeps its bloom, as I my love will save
     All for my grave."

In the wild autumn weather a dread sword slipped from its sheath;
While the boughs sobbed together, I fought a fight with Death,
And I vanquished him with prayer, and I vanquished him by faith:
Now the summer air is sweet with the rose's fragrant breath
     That conquered Death.

LOVE

True love is that which never can be lost:
Though cast away, alone and ownerless,
Like a strayed child that, wandering, misses most
When night comes down its mother's last caress,

True love dies not when banished and forgot.
But, solitary, barters still with Heaven
The scanty share of joy cast in its lot
For joys to the beloved freely given.

Love smiling stands afar to watch and see
Each blessing it has bought, like angel's kiss,
Fall on the loved one's face, who ne'er may know
At what strange cost thus, overflowingly,
His cup is filled, or how its depth of bliss
Doth give the measure of another's woe.

THE WILD GEESE

I had no sail to cross the sea,
A brave white bird went forth from me,
My heart was hid beneath his wing:
O strong white bird, come back in spring!

I watched the wild geese rise and cry
Across the flaring western sky;
Their winnowing pinions clove the light,
Then vanished, and came down the night.

I laid me low, my day was done,
I longed not for the morrow's sun,
But closely swathed in swoon of sleep.
Forgot to hope, forgot to weep.

The moon, through veils of gloomy red,
A warm yet dusky radiance shed
All down our valley's golden stream,
And flushed my slumber with a dream.

Her mystic torch lit up my brain;
My spirit rose and lived amain,
And followed through the windy spray

That bird upon its watery way.

"O wild white bird, O wait for me!
My soul hath wings to fly with thee:
On foam waves, lengthening out afar,
We'll ride toward the western star.

"O'er glimmering plains, through forest gloom,
To track a wanderer's feet I come;
'Mid lonely swamp, by haunted brake,
I'll pass unfrighted for his sake.

"Alone, afar, his footsteps roam,
The stars his roof, the tent his home.
Saw'st thou what way the wild geese flew
To sunward through the thick night dew?

"Carry my soul where he abides.
And pierce the mystery that hides
His presence, and through time and space
Look with mine eyes upon his face."

Beside his prairie fire he rests,
All feathered things are in their nests:
"What strange wild bird is this," he saith,
"Still fragrant with the ocean's breath?

"Perch on my hand, thou briny thing,
And let me stroke thy shy wet wing;
What message in thy soft eye thrills?
I see again my native hills,

"And vale, the river's silver streak.
The mist upon the blue, blue peak,
The shadows grey, the golden sheaves,
The mossy walls, the russet eaves.

"I greet the friends I've loved and lost,
Do all forget? No, tempest-tost.
That braved for me the ocean's foam,
Some heart remembers me at home.

"Ere spring's return I will be there,
Thou strange sea-fragrant messenger!"
I wake and weep; the moon shines sweet,
O dream too short! O bird too fleet!

IF

Deep in the grave I lie, and feel no pain
Who suffered so much woe among the flowers,
And in the sun-kissed fields of tall ripe grain,
That hide me now alike from heats and showers.
Deep in the grave I lie,
No more to die.
Or dread the footfall of appalling hours.

I see no more the red and white of joy
That lives in roses and the eastern skies;
My folded hands know not the sad employ
Of sending forth a heart's rich argosies
Out on the shining main;
No more again
My ears can hear the strife of drowning cries.

If bird glad of its mate, or man's sad heart,
Could taste the peace of lying here so still,
No music had the world, no fires of art
By bliss and anguish fed, by good and ill,
On a cold earth could burn.
All life would turn,
And hasten here below to sleep its fill.

STOWAWAYS

O wide-winged ship, out of a distant port,
The winds are with thee and the seas run white,
Hope-breathing winds and seas of wild delight: —
Thy prow can cut a thousand moments short!

Let mists enshroud thee, and let tempests wail
O'er treacherous rocks that haste to rise and rend
Thy trusty breast, thou'lt win the happy end;
Thou bearest on thy mast a charmed sail.

Three stowaways are hid within thy hold,
And storms may rage, and blinding mists may scare.
And spectral icebergs spread their glittering snare;
Sail on, O wide-winged ship, with freight of gold!

Lie, if thou wilt, for lost in cavern wave,
And greet the splendid berg with shuddering kiss:

Thou'rt sure as sunrise, safe as souls in bliss;
The harbour waits thee — not an ocean grave.

Now, when thy broad brave wings are drooping furled,
And all thy costly cargo pours ashore,
Rich spices, and fair fabrics, silver ore,
And burning rubies from a far-off world,

Will silent steal away the stowaways, —
My heart and its two angels, love and faith,
That lived in thee and prayed, 'twixt death and death,
And sailed thee into port of golden days.

TWO STRANGERS

Two strangers at my door in the cool eve,
After the sun and long before the moon,
On the dun moorland where I sleep and weave,
Night, noon, and morning — morning, night, and noon.

Content I wove my web, and dreamless slept.
With wild thyme, and the wind, and lark sweet-shrill,
With warm wide eyes that neither burned nor wept,
And feet that knew no pit and climbed no hill.

My home was but a tent full whitely spread.
Of angels' wings with rifts of light between;
A little cold, but safe from all things dread,
And sweet with echoes from a world unseen.

Lo, those two strangers! and from two there fell
One shadow that did seem to make a third,
An awful thing, whereof I could not tell
Whether 'twere man or woman, beast or bird.

The first, with dazzling face full turned on me,
Gave me the glory of her radiant eyes,
And touch of her fair hands that moved with glee,
And laughed upon my looks of glad surprise.

The second, with sad mien and face avert,
Like one unwelcome stood, and made no sign,
While came I forth with eye and step alert
To bid both enter and be guests of mine.

Spake the first stranger, "Choose 'twixt her and me.

Who may not bide together. Sweet am I.
But drive her hence, who cometh but to be
Disturber of delicious harmony."

The other murmured, "Though I am not fair,
Take me, and let her go, who will but stay
Only to put her footprint on thy stair,
Like shifting sunbeam in a windy May.

"With her I enter not, but when she goes
I follow surely, and upon my tread
A fiend who lurks behind us two, and knows
How to possess thee when we two are fled.

"But if I enter only, I will prove
Thy trusty comrade, and thy soul shall know
The heights of faith, the width and depth of love;
Despair comes not though I may never go."

I turned my face from her who looked delight;
Her smile dissolved away o'er moor and mere;
While the foul fiend went howling towards the night.
I gave my hand to Sorrow, She is here.

THE CHILDREN OF LIR

Mournfully, O mournfully,
The waves of Moyle run to the sea;
White their lips that ever mutter
Of a tale they long to utter.
Softly sleep, my Fionnula!

Never more thy sad wings trailing,
Through the rack of tempests wailing,
Helpless in thine anguish human,
Weary swan and hapless woman! —
Fionnula, O Ulula!

Mighty Lir, why hast thou taken
To thy widowed breast forsaken
(Softly sleep, my Fionnula!)
One to hate thy children tender,
So that Lucifer may lend her
Power to steal from thine embraces
Curling heads and blooming faces?
Fionnula, O Ulula!

Mournfully, O mournfully,
The waves of Moyle run to the sea.
"Laughing girl, awake so early,
Rise and deck thy beauty rarely."
(Softly sleep, my Fionnula!)
"Hear my voice that is thy mother's;
Rise, and call thy gentle brothers;
We will journey all together
Through the pleasant summer weather —"
Fionnula, O Ulula!

"To thy grandsire, lone and aged,
In his distant palace caged,"
(Softly sleep, my Fionnula!)
"We will travel through the sunshine.
You shall kiss him in the moonshine,
He will stroke your flowing tresses.
Smiling at your young caresses,"
Fionnula, O Ulula!

Sullenly and mournfully
The waves of Moyle run to the sea.
"Mother, what is this dark water?"
"Let us tarry by it, daughter!"
(Softly sleep, my Fionnula!)
"In its wilds of lake and river,
Tarry thou a swan for ever,
All your happy words are spoken,
All your girlhood's promise broken,"
Fionnula, O Ulula!

"Take thy brothers with thee yonder;
So for ever may ye wander"
(Softly sleep, my Fionnula!)
"Till the sound of sweet bells ringing,
Reach your ears, a message bringing;
Long your hearts shall burn to hear it,
Long 'twill be ere I shall fear it! "
Fionnula, O Ulula!

Mournfully, O mournfully,
The waves of Moyle run to the sea.
Eire's princess, Lir's sweet daughter,
Breasts the dark and lonely water;
(Softly sleep, my Fionnula!)
Three wild swans drift out together,
Through the blue and sunny weather.

Drooping wings and heads that languish,
Sickening with their human anguish —
Fionnula, O Ulula!

"Oh, my brothers, keep beside me,
Lest the rolling wave divide me,"
(Softly sleep, my Fionnula!)
"From your tender woe and weakness,
Little brothers, and your meekness,
Let my braver eyes behold you,
And my stronger wings enfold you!"
Fionnula, O Ulula!

Mournfully, O mournfully,
The waves of Movie run to the sea.
"Here arc lilies golden-headed,
Unto white companions wedded;"
(Softly sleep, my Fionnula!)
"Let us rest amid their sweetness—
No, the curse in its completeness
Keeps us ever shifting, shifting.
Three wild swans for ever drifting!"
Fionnula, O Ulula!

Sluggish years, how slow your motion.
Rolling in the rolling ocean,
(Softly sleep, my Fionnula!)
To the dirge of Moyle's dark water,
Breaking over Lir's sad daughter.
Rising, falling, ebbing, flowing,
Slowly coming, slowly going—
Fionnula, O Ulula!

O stormily and mournfully
The waves of Moyle foam to the sea;
Winter blasts come forth to meet them,
Bitterly the whirlwinds greet them,
(Softly sleep, my Fionnula!)
Side by side for ever clinging
'Gainst the tempest, panting, winging,
Seeking by the lake's white edges
Shelter 'mid the whistling sedges—
Fionnula, O Ulula!

Seasons coming, seasons going,
Times have changed beyond our knowing,
(Softly sleep, my Fionnula!)
Lir hath mourned himself to madness,

Death hath ta'en away his sadness,
Now another hath his glory,
And forgotten is thy story,
Fionnula, O Ulula!

Mournfully, O mournfully,
The waves of Moyle sob in the sea.
Fishers on the green bank yonder.
Stay their hands and gaze in wonder
(Softly sleep, my Fionnula!)
Where amid the breakers striving.
Beaten by the rain-winds driving.
Greyly gleam the three together.
Phantom creatures, hurrying — whither?
Fionnula, Ulula!

Like our dreams, confused and broken,
Pass the years till God hath spoken.
(Softly sleep, my Fionnula!)
From our mountains and our meadows
Move at last the morning shadows.
Comes the banisher of sadness,
Comes the messenger of gladness,
Fionnula, O Ulula!

Dreamfully and mournfully
The waves of Moyle rock in the sea.
Hark, the sound of seraphs singing
Like the chime of sweet bells ringing!
(Softly sleep, my Fionnula!)
Comes a ship across the ocean,
Winging with an angel's motion,
Bearing one whose words of wonder
Rend the clouds of woe asunder,
Fionnula, O Ulula!

Hark, the sound of children singing!
Hark, the chime of sweet bells ringing
(Softly sleep, my Fionnula!)
See the fair procession filing
Through the woods and pastures smiling,
White-robed creatures, loved, forgiven,
Newly washed in dews from heaven.
Fionnula, O Ulula!

Peacefully, O peacefully.
The waves of Moyle sleep in the sea.
Banners flying, censers swinging.

Peace on earth brave men are singing,
(Softly sleep, my Fionnula!)
Holy Patrick, pardon bearing.
Far in front the cross up-rearing,
To the winds their Master nameth,
To the hills their Lord proclaimeth,
Fionnula, O Ulula!

Ring the bells, O ring them clearly,
Ring them late and ring them early,
(Softly sleep, my Fionnula!)
Through the sun and through the shadow,
O'er the moorland and the meadow,
Lakes, and streams, and rocky places,
And the sandy sea-girt spaces!
Fionnula, O Ulula!

Mournfully, O mournfully,
The waves of Moyle run to the sea.
Let the sound go roaming, roaming,
"Hark, the Lord of love is coming! "
(Softly sleep, my Fionnula!)
Fling it far across the water
To the ear of Lir's sad daughter;
Ring it louder, ring it clearer,
"All ye stricken ones, draw nearer!"
Fionnula, O Ulula!

Now upon the wave-girt heather
Saint and flock have knelt together,
(Softly sleep, my Fionnula!)
O'er the voice of their appealing,
What is this strange music stealing?
"'Tis the swan!" a fisher crieth,
"Swan that singeth while she dieth"—
Fionnula, O Ulula!

Mournfully, O mournfully,
The waves of Moyle run to the sea.
Lo! the phantom three appearing,
Far away, yet nearing, nearing,
(Softly sleep, my Fionnula!)
Three grey forms with pinions dragging.
Winging feebly, panting, flagging,
Beaten by the outward breaker,
Battling, ever weaker, weaker —
Fionnula, O Ulula!

To the shore the waters sweep them;
Well may tender spirits weep them,
(Softly sleep, my Fionnula!)
Surely these are human creatures,
Broken forms and wasted features;
On the beach behold them lying,
Faintly breathing, slowly dying,
Fionnula, O Ulula!

Mournfully, O mournfully,
The waves of Moyle run to the sea;
Bathe them in the hallowing water —
Lir's brave sons and Lir's sweet daughter.
(Softly sleep, my Fionnula!)
Dig the grave, and kindly lay them
Where no waves nor winds affray them.
Never more their sad wings trailing
Through the rack of tempests wailing,
Fionnula, O Ulula!

Plant the cross of Christ above them,
Bid the little children love them,
(Softly sleep, my Fionnula!)
While at eve they cease their playing,
Dimpled cheeks together laying.
Listening to the wind-bells ringing,
"Hark!" they say, "the swans are singing!"
Fionnula, Ulula!

A SLEEPING HOMESTEAD

The meadows slumber fair beneath the moon,
While wakes the watchful river at their feet,
And all the air is filled with odours sweet,
The breath of flowers that will unfold full soon.

In mazy mystery the forest hides,
And straggling trees have caught a sylvan grace;
The sleeping farm-house shows its placid face
Between the shadows where the grove divides.

Still are the sparrows nested in the thatch,
And still the callow larks beneath the brake;
The startled doves with tender coo awake
As bays the moon-struck mastiff on his watch.

Now warmer light upon the welkin lies,
And deeper night intensifies the peace;
Only the river moves and will not cease
Its swift, up-searching glances to the skies.

By blooming white-thorn and by climbing rose,
I know the nook where dreams the maiden sweet;
Honest her heart as sheaves of goodly wheat,
Fairer her face than any flower that blows.

I know the chamber where the old folks rest,
With hearts at peace and all their labour done;
Where ruddy children sleep till shines the sun.
Where breathes the baby, warm in mother's breast.

I know the barn where safe from midnight chill
The weary beggar snores amid the hay.
Waiting the first red warning of the day
To grasp his staff and cross the distant hill.

God hath the simple homestead in His eye,
And sometimes in a solemn hour like this
He sheds about it dreams of promised bliss.
With mellow moonlight from the summer sky.

THE NIGHTINGALES

June roses ripen through the land,
All red and white and paly gold;
Green shadows veil them where they stand,
Their breathing scents the sunlit wold.
The roses glow, but what avails?
I do not hear the nightingales.

The woods lie under some sweet spell,
Their mossy lanes are dim with light,
Ensilvered is the marble well.
Deep summer walketh through the night
Walketh awake; yet something ails
My soul; I want the nightingales,

Soft summer night, fair summer day,
Of leaping light, of dreamful shade,
Who that hath lived through you shall say
Which for the fuller bliss was made?
Yet aches my heart; my spirit fails —

O May, give back the nightingales!

GIRLHOOD AT MIDNIGHT

Thou art not coming, sleep; then hie away,
And let my leaping thoughts be quit of thee.
The moon hath teemed upon my chamber floor
A rain of tender light from Paradise;
And round my casement, yawning to the blue,
The stirring breathing passion-flowerets cling:
It is too fair a night to swoon away,
And lie unconscious till the lark's aloft!

From out my little bed I step herewith,
And leave its gleaming whiteness in the shades;
I will go forth, and walk with shining feet
Under the moon, and hear the nightingales.
Jug, jug, tirroo, tirroo! O sweet, my heart.
But listen, listen to the voice of love,
Singing in dreams from out the gloom of leaves:
The red rose is awake and listening too!

O lady rose, O sister, fragrant, sweet,
Thou dost not know what now I tell thee true,
That yesterday he likened me to thee,
And praised my damask cheek and called me fair.

Jug, jug, tirroo, tirroo! he called me fair
That ne'er was fair unto myself before,
So I am safely housed within a heart,
Sweet rose, as that dew-drop is housed in thine!

Now I have banished sleep, and come alive
To whisper thee my news in this still hour —
Thou and the moon, no other hath my tale;
And mind thou dost not tell it to the sun,
Or any prying creature winging by.
My secret I will keep another day —
Then all the world can wonder at my joy!

A DREADED HOUR

I looked one morn with a peering eye.
Along the far reaches of earth and sky,

And out of the mists of futurity
I saw an hour that was travelling towards me.

Its form was gloomy, and sad, and weird,
And my heart within me grew sore afeard;
Oh, why through the mists of the morning dim
Did I search and seek for a shape so grim?

I dreamed in the night of its noiseless tread,
And wakened at morning and cried and prayed:
"O God, give me courage, and God, give me power
When I shall go forth and shall meet that hour!"

For quick in the meadow and slow through the wood,
And swift on the river and strong in the flood.
And climbing the mountain and swimming the sea,
I knew that dark hour was travelling towards me.

So its shadow fell on my summer days,
And its menace frightened my peaceful ways;
In the song of the bird and the bloom of the flower
I knew but the dread of that darksome hour.

I said, "O my heart, thou must quick forget
This gloomy cause of thy fear and fret;
Arise and mix in the brilliant strife.
And carol and dance at the feast of life!"

But in pause of dance and in break of song
The fear with me grew wild and strong,
And long remembrance was lighter pain
Than forgetting and calling to mind again.

Then made I a cell for my timorous heart
Where I and my terror lived all apart;
Till my soul grew stronger with thought and prayer,
For the Saviour of life He looked on me there.

The years went by and the hour drew near.
And kneeling I said, "It will soon be here!"
And my soul fell down in the swoon of death
When I heard its heart-beat and felt its breath!

I cried, "O God, give me strength and power,
For I must go forth and meet that hour!"
And I went and stood in my rightful place —
Till it raised its veil and looked in my face.

It raised the veil and it gazed on me;
And my soul leaped up into ecstasy,
(O, the Lord of life he is strange and good!)
For the face of an angel was under its hood.

MY BLACKBIRD

In the sycamore tree, in the sycamore tree,
There is a blackbird that sings to me;
Sweet is his note as the rose in June,
Quainter than any old poet's rune,
Wild as the water that wanders o'er
Hill and dale to a far seashore;—
Softly, oh! softly he says his say,
'Twixt the dawn and day, 'twixt the dawn and day!

Oh! in the sycamore tree, in the sycamore tree,
There lives for ever a wonder to me:
Out of a small winged creature's throat,
In a warbling, murmuring, marvellous note,
Cometh the utterance, deep and low,
Of the human love that is bliss or woe.
Oh! in the sycamore tree, in the sycamore tree,
How can a bird speak so to me?

When the sun is high he will not sing,
As love were such a holy, bashful thing;
But just when the dawn begins to break,
And soul and sense are but half awake,
It tunes on the air that mystical song,
A little now, and more ere long —
Oh! with notes that are tender, and strange, and deep,
Calling my heart through the mists of sleep.

Yet nested high in that bow'ring tree.
What can a little bird know of me?
Hath he studied life from his home of leaves
Through open windows on summer eves?
Or is it a secret unguessed, unknown,
That he hath a human heart of his own.
With the rapturous bliss of its joyous mood —
Its swoonings, yearnings, and tears of blood?

Oh! since first that little bird spake to me,
A joy, and a grief, and a mystery
Have perched and nested deep in my heart,

Where one must remain when two depart.
And my spirit knows not which of the three
Will stay and for ever abide with me:
But the bird he knoweth and singeth alway
'Twixt the dawn and day, 'twixt the dawn and day.

MY SAINT

I see a convent gray —
It standeth above the town;
It looketh from the distant way
Like a monk in his faded gown.

The town is older and grayer
That sitteth below its feet;
And sin, and pain, and sorrow, and care,
Are dwelling in every street.

Dwelling in every street.
Yet hurried from place to place,
As the Sisters go with their burden sweet,
Bread, and comfort, and grace.

In a nook of that convent gray
She dwelleth, my tender Saint;
Sweeter her face than I can say.
Nobler than word can paint.

Her wimple is white as milk,
Her robe is coarse and spare;
While never a lady in gems and silk
Looked half so grand and fair.

Her mind is a river of light,
Her heart is a well of love;
But none may look on her soul so white
Save only the Lord above.

That soul's most rapid flame —
The soul of my tender Saint —
It wasteth sore her beautiful frame,
And maketh her body faint.

She stayeth her eager feet
And goeth not oft to the town;
But up in her window, lone and sweet,

She sitteth, and gazeth down.

O crowded, sad gray walls,
O people who dwell within,
Little ye know of the tear that falls
Day by day for your sin!

Her town is her nested dove —
She huggeth it close and dear;
She wrappeth it round with motherly love,
She watcheth with motherly fear.

They turn, the godless men,
They turn their steps and they come;
They know not why, but they come again,
As this were their childhood's home.

They turn with willing feet,
The foolish wife and maid;
They have no fear of the lips so sweet,
That preach, but never upbraid.

They come, with blushing face;
And they come, with tearful eye;
And one hath sorrow, and one disgrace,
To whisper when none are by.

And kneeling close to her knee
They catch her fire, I ween;
And, burning strangely and holily,
Are not what they have been.

She hath them all in her heart,
It is deep, and strong, and broad —
And well I know with what loving art
She talketh of them to God.

AUTUMN SONG

Close the door and drop the latch,
Light the log and mend the thatch,
Look no more to see the shadow
Of the beech-tree on the meadow.
Sit you by the hearth to-day;
Come in, come in, for the swallow's away.

No more piping round the eaves,
Housed are all the golden sheaves.
Like to birds of brilliant feather
Scarlet leaflets fly together,
Drift and drop like hopes foregone;
Come in, come in, for the swallow has flown!

Misty woods look far from home,
Playful streams grow quarrelsome.
Now your eye will gladly follow
Smoke wreaths curling in the hollow.
Strong of heart and sweet of mouth,
Come! — and the swallow may stay in the south!

GOOD-NIGHT

The dear one hath gone in at her gate,
In at the gate of her home —
Little birds, little birds, ye need not wait,
Hither again she will not come.

The sun hath fitted a golden bar
Blazing across her lintel red;
The lilies down in the river bed
Expect the evening star.

The longing trees are wishing, wishing.
Soft good-nights at the window pane;
And swift, all fainter murmurs hushing,
Lovingly patters the summer rain.

The holy corner, the happy home,
It keepeth her counsel sweet;
Hie hence, hie hence, ye lingering feet!
Hither again she will not come.

AFTER THE WAR

The summer has come back again, I feel
The sunshine cover me from brow to feet;
The bee goes searching for his honeyed meal,
The rose is crimson-dyed and smells full sweet.

The lily looks as stately and serene

As in the day ere I began to grieve;
The stream is musical, the forest green;
The faithless nightingales sing loud at eve.

Why now should flow'rets deck the blood-stained ground?
O blooming rose! O cruel flaunting thing,
That wear'st the colour of my love's death wound!
O birds that know him dead and yet will sing!

The plum is hanging on the southern wall,
It waxeth ripe beneath the sun's warm ray;
Last year we did not wait for it to fall,
But plucked its sweetness as we went our way.

Now let it roll and wither into mould,
Like that dear hand that dropped away from mine;
Since so much life is silenced and grown cold
'Tis good to rot while star and sunbeam shine.

For o'er our sun there came a cloud of gloom,
When shout of war was blown across the lea:
To thee, my love, it was the trump of doom:
It was the trump of doom to thee and me.

Now all return that shared our joy before,
Of flower and sunshine, bough and singing bird;
Only thy footstep cometh back no more,
Only thy voice shall not again be heard.

The summer has come back, but not for me:
I do not even know thy place of rest.
Or useless flowers might win some sanctity,
By shedding bloom above so brave a breast.

Somewhere the grass is springing o'er thy head,
And so I'll love the grass and hold it sweet;
And when, content, at last I too am dead,
I'll have no other covering for my feet

Upon my heart shall lie no sculptured stone,
No idle wreath above my brow shall twine;
The tender grass shall wave o'er me alone:
Only the breeze shall know thy grave and mine.

THE BUILDERS

I saw the builders laying
Stones on the grassy sod,
And people praised them, saying:
"A fane to the mighty God
Shall rise aloft in glory,
Pillars and arches wide,
Windows stained with the story
Of Christ the Crucified."

I saw the broken boulders
Lie in the waving grass,
Flung down from bending shoulders.
And said, "Our lives must pass
Ere wide cathedral spreading
Can' span this mossy field
Where kine are slowly treading
And flowers their honey yield.

"Oh, dreaming builders, tarry!
Unchain your souls from toil,
Leave the rock in the quarry,
The bloom upon the soil;
For life is short, my brothers, —
And labour wastes it sore, —
Why toil to gladden others
When you shall breathe no more?

"Oh! come with footstep springing,
With empty hands and free.
And tread the green earth singing
'The world was made for me! '
Pray amid nature's sweetness
In pillared forest glade.
Content with the incompleteness
Of fanes that the Lord has made!"

The builders, never heeding.
Kept piling stone on stone.
Their hands with toil were bleeding —
I went my way alone.
Prayed in the forest temple
And ate the wild-bee's store;
My life was pure and simple —
What would the Lord have more?

The years, like one long morning,
They all flew swiftly by;
Old age with little warning

Came creeping softly nigh.
Now (be we all forgiven!)
I longed to see, alas!
What the builders had raised to heaven
Instead of the tender grass.

I heard a sweet bell ringing
Over the world so wide;
I heard a sound of singing
Across the eventide.
What sight my soul bewilders
Beneath the sunset's glow?
The fane that the dreaming builders
Were building long ago!

'Tis not the sculptured portal,
Or windows jewelled wide,
With joys of the life immortal,
And woes of Him who died.
That fill my soul with wonder,
And drain my heart of tears.
And ask with voice of thunder,
"Where are thy wasted years!"

But a thousand thousand creatures
Kneel down where grew the sod.
And hear with glowing features
The words that breathe of God.
Alone and empty-handed,
I wait by the open door:
Such work hath the Lord commanded,
And I can work — no more!

The builders, never heeding,
They lie and take their rest.
And hands no longer bleeding
Are folded on each breast —
The grass waves o'er them sleeping,
And flowerets red and white,
Where I kneel above them weeping,
And whisper, "You were right."

CAST OUT!

The moon is red and low, and the stars are few,
The city moaneth like one who talks in his sleep,

In distant meadows full heavily falls the dew,
The dew in the city it falleth from eyes that weep.

Now is the time, my soul, when a grieving pain,
Frightened away by the eyes that shine in the day,
May dare to come forth awhile, and be free again,
And look in thy face and say what it hath to say.

Its mien is pure and true, and it seemeth calm
Though deep in its gaze there is lying the gloom of death;
Its murmur sounds like the holiest heavenly psalm.
But it singeth a siren's song to thy dreaming faith.

Let it come forth and utter its plaintive moan,
Listened so oft that thine ears are growing dull
To sounds less sad and soft, to the cheerful tone
That rings in the chord of life when it swelleth full.

Hearken it now for the past and never more,
Heed not the eyes that crave and the hand that dings,
Kiss it once at the future's glimmering door.
Float it away in the dark on its own sad wings.

So shall it reach that realm on the verge of night,
Where shadows of fair false things and their echoes be;
Thy way is across the hills in the kindling light
'Mid living souls with a footstep glad and free!

THE FAITHFUL LIGHT

There's a light in the cottage window —
It shines far over the vale;
The sun is gone and the day is done.
And the stars are few and pale.

Only a farthing rushlight,
With feeble flickering ray —
'Twill gleam and wane in that window-pane
Till wears the night away.

A woman sits in the cottage
And weeps and tends the light;
Her loving care has placed it there
To glimmer the livelong night.

For one to sea went sailing,

And one will sure come back;
The light must burn till he return
By the lonely beaten track.

He comes not over the mountain,
He comes not across the vale;
The beacon-light keeps burning bright,
Though the woman's face is pale.

He lies deep down in the ocean —
But others cross the plain,
And hearts beat high when passing nigh
That light in the window-pane.

They bless the faithful watcher —
The heart that will not break,
The friendly light in the darksome night
That burns for another's sake.

Her face grows paler and paler —
But wanderers reach their home
Her loving pain is not in vain
Though one will never come.

WILFULNESS AND PATIENCE

I said, "I am going into the garden,
Into the flush of the sweetness of life;
I can stay in the wilderness no longer,
Where sorrow and sickness and pain are so rife

So I shod my feet in their golden sandals.
And looped my gown with a ribbon of blue,
And into the garden went I singing,
The birds in the boughs fell a-singing too.

Just at the wicket I met with Patience.
Grave was her face, and pure, and kind;
But oh, I loved not her ashen mantle,
Such sober looks were not to my mind.

Said Patience, "Go not into the garden,
But come with me by the difficult ways.
Over the wastes and the wilderness mountains.
To the higher levels of love and praise!"

Gaily I laughed as I opened the wicket,
And Patience, pitying, flitted away;
The garden glory was full of the morning —
The morning changed to the glamour of day.

O sweet were the winds among my tresses,
And sweet the flowers that bent at my knees,
Ripe were the fruits that fell at my wishing,
But sated soon was my soul with these.

And would I were hand in hand with Patience,
Tracking her feet on the difficult ways.
Over the wastes and the wilderness mountains,
To the higher levels of love and praise!

CHRIST, THE GLEANER

In a vision of the night
Looked I upon fields of light,
Spreading broad beneath the moon,
Fair as though the night were noon.

Moonlight fell on golden sheaves,
Woven as the reaper weaves;
Bounteous harvest gathered there
Hath repaid the Master's care.

All His toilers soundly sleep,
One alone doth vigil keep;
Who is this that cometh last
Where the reaper's feet have passed?

One who walketh grave and slow.
Going as the gleaners go,
Stooping oft full tenderly,
That no grain escape his eye;

Gathering in secluded spot
What the gleaners have forgot;
In His mantle deep and wide
Many a broken stalk doth hide.

Ere the morning shall arise,
Christ, the Gleaner, with His prize
Maketh goodly sheaf and crown
Out of what was trodden down.

Bruised and broken, held unsound.
Left to rot upon the ground, —
E'en the wisest gleaner saw
Nothing there but worthless straw.

Only He with eyes of light
Pierced beyond our mortal sight;
In the sullied husk He knew
Living grain was hid from view.

Lo! it is the darkest hour.
Stars have set and clouds do lower;
Christ, the Gleaner, gleaneth still,
Casting radiance where He will.

When the sun shall flood the land.
And the golden sheaves shall stand.
Ripened for the Harvest-home,
Waiting till the Master come:

Riper, fuller, none than they
Trodden once into the clay;
Gleaned from dust by hand Divine,
In eternal light they shine.

LAMENT OF THE RIVER

Mourns the river: — I came down from the mountain,
Jubilant with pride and glee,
Leaping through the winds, and shouting
That I had an errand to the sea!

The rocks stood against me, and we wrestled,
But I leaped from the holding of their hands, —
Leaped from their holding, and went slipping
And sliding into lower lands.

I carolled as I went, and the woodlands
Smiled as my song murmured by.
And the birds on the wing heard me singing,
And dropped mc a blessing from the sky.

The flowers on the bank heard me singing,
And the buds that had been red and sweet
Grew redder and sweeter as they listened.

And their golden hearts began to beat.

The cities through their din heard me passing,
They came out and crowned me with their towers;
The trees hung their garlands up above me,
And coaxed me to rest among their bowers.

But I laughed as I left them in the sunshine:
There was never aught of rest for me
Till I mingled my waters with the ocean,
Till I sang in the chorus of the sea.

Ah me! for my pride upon the mountain,
Ah me! for my beauty in the plains,
Where my crest floated glorious in the sunshine.
And the clouds showered strength into my veins.

Alas! for the blushing little blossoms.
And the grasses with their long golden drifts,
For the shadows of the forest in the noontide.
And the full-handed cities with their gifts.

I have mingled my waters with the ocean,
I have sung in the chorus of the sea.
And my soul from the tumult of the billows
Will never more be jubilant and free.

I sing, but the echo of my mourning
Returns to me, shrieking back again
One wild weak note amongst the myriads
That are sobbing 'neath the thunders of the main.

Oh well for the dewdrop on die go wan,
Oh well for the pool upon the height,
Where the kids gather thirsty in the noontide,
And stars watch all through the summer night,

There is no home-returning for the waters
To the mountain, whence they came glad and free;
There is no happy ditty for the singer
That has sung in the chorus of the sea.

NEWS TO TELL

Neighbour, lend me your arm, for I am not well,
This wound you see is scarcely a fortnight old.

All for a sorry message I had to tell,
I've travelled many a mile in wet and cold.

Yon is the old grey chateau above the road.
He bade me seek it, my comrade brave and gay
Stately forest and river so brown and broad,
He showed me the scene as he a-dying lay.

I have been there, and, neighbour, I am not well;
I bore his sword and some of his curling hair,
Knocked at the gate and said I had news to tell,
Entered a chamber and saw his mother there.

Tall and straight with the snows of age on her head.
Brave and stern as a soldier's mother might be,
Deep in her eyes a living look of the dead,
She grasped her staff and silently gazed at me.

I thought I'd better be dead than meet her eye;
She guessed it all, I'd never a word to tell.
Taking the sword in her arms she heaved a sigh,
Clasping the curl in her hand she sobbed, and fell.

I raised her up; she sate in her stately chair,
Her face like death, but not a tear in her eye;
We heard a step, and tender voice on the stair
Murmuring soft to an infant's cooing cry.

My lady she sate erect, and sterner grew,
Finger on mouth she motioned me not to stay;
A girl came in, the wife of the dead I knew,
She held his babe, and, neighbour, I fled away!

I tried to run, but I heard the widow's cry.
Neighbour, I have been hurt and I am not well:
I pray to God that never until I die
May I again have such sorry news to tell.

A STOLEN VISIT

When you are wrapped in happy sleep,
I walk about your house by night,
With many a wistful, stealthy peep
At what I've loved by morning light.

Your head is on the pillow laid,

My feet are where your footsteps were;
Your soul to other lands has strayed.
My heart can hear you breathe and stir.

I seat me in your wonted chair.
And ope your book a little space;
I touch the flowers that knew your care.
The mirror that reflects your face.

I kiss the pen that spoke your thought,
The spot whereon you knelt to pray,
The message with your wisdom fraught
Writ down on paper yesterday,

The garment that you lately wore,
The threshold that your step goes by,
The music that you fingered o'er,
The picture that contents your eye.

Yet when you wake from happy sleep,
And, busy here, and busy there,
You take your wonted morning peep
At what is good and what is fair,

"She has been here," you will not say,
My prying face you will not find;
You'll think, "She is a mile away,"
My love hath left no mark behind.

A SECRET

I have a secret to tell.
Shall I cry it aloud to the wind
That it ring forth like a bell
And leave not an echo behind
On the wind?

Shall I shout it from the shore,
Through the bay of the deep-mouthed wave,
That it drown in the breaker's roar,
And toss in a stormy grave
'Neath the wave?

To the bloom of new-blown flowers
Shall I trust it, as sweet as they,
That it perish after the showers

Defaced and defiled in a day
E'en as they?

Shall I dig a hole full deep
And bury it under the moor,
That it rise from troubled sleep
And Cometh again to my door
From the moor?

Shall I tell it my friend in youth
That he turn, unhearing, away,
And it fall dead from my mouth —
Dead until the Judgment Day —
Cast away.

My secret, still silent lie;
I too am dead when thou art.
Now, quick, if thou wilt, and die,
But die where thou art, in my heart,
Where thou art!

THE DENIAL OF PETER

I tell thee, silly maid, I know him not.
Go, let me rest my weary limbs awhile,
And warm my fingers chill before the blaze.
No longer turn on me thy mocking gaze,
Making these people wag their heads and smile:
If e'er I saw the man, I have forgot!

So said I, and the maid passed, and the crowd.
I stooped above the fire in lonely gloom;
With my cold cowardice I sat apart,
The lie lay heavy on my aching heart,
As, o'er faint murmurs from the council-room,
I heard black oaths, and laughter fierce and loud.

O'erwhelmed with grief, and weariness, and wrath,
My soul was sunk in stupor dull and deep.
Why had I left my boat upon the tide,
My simple home, the sunny lake beside.
The noontide task, the long night's peaceful sleep.
For these wild scenes, portending shame and death?

A yell arose, out burst the raging crowd
Like a dark river from the Chamber's mouth.

And one pale face came silent through the din,
Gleaming with grief, paused, looked upon my sin:
Mirrored I saw it in the eyes of Truth,
And as He passed, I fled, and shrieked aloud.

Out in the dawn the cock was crowing faint
Across the dreaming fields and up the hills;
All nature wakened sweetly from her sleep.
While I, heart-broken, could but weep and weep.
O Master! Friend! oh, let me share Thine ills,
Make me Thy servant, bondman, martyr, saint!

SNOW AND FAMINE

What are you weaving, silent Snow?
To and fro, sad and slow,
While the winds are keening low,
Weird and low, thick with woe;
Hoarse and sudden, sobbing loud,
Shrill with woe. Ah! I know.
Well I know, you weave a shroud,
Mournful Snow!

What are you hiding, eerie Snow?
Pallid so, crouching low,
With your trailing garment's flow,
Spread beneath the moon's pale glow.
What do you hide, so cold and dread,
Down below? Ah! I know.
You swathe the lone unburied dead,
Ghastly Snow!

Where do you drift, mysterious Snow?
To and fro, sad and slow,
While the rough winds gasp with woe,
Through the cabin door you go,
Treading over the hearth and floor,
Lying low. Yes, I know,
The home-blaze leaps there never more,
Chilly Snow!

Is it Christmas, wandering Snow?
To and fro, roaming so;
We in the mountains cannot know,
Sunk in woe, dying slow.
Is the Saviour born on earth?

Ah! 'tis so; yes, I know,
We'll warm us at His heavenly hearth,
Kindly Snow!

LULLABY

Lullaby sweet, my baby love,
For the dew is on the rose;
Mother will rock her treasure, singing,
Till the drooping eye-lids close.
The slim white angels are winging, winging,
Down from the silver moon, O
Lullaby sweet, my baby bird.
While mother will rock and croon.

The wild wood-doves in the oaks above
Are cooing soft in their dreams,
And the drowsy air a whisper is holding
With the sleepy mountain streams.
Deep in the pool the lily golden
Is closing her brilliant eyes, O
Lullaby sweet, my baby dear,
For the stars flash out in the skies!

Lullaby sweet, my babe of pearl;
Now close, my lily flower!
The thrush has forgot his music mellow,
The blackbird's asleep in his bower.
On mother's bosom is made thy pillow,
Her love sweet watch will keep, O
Rocked in her arms, till sunrise hour
Sleep softly — sleep, oh! sleep.

LENT

Comes the quiet time of year —
Now the gray road doth appear
Which reluctant feet must tread
Amidst the ashes of the dead, —

Gray and chill, yet safe and sure,
Fringed with snowdrops pale and pure
Underneath a sky that grieves
O'er barren, boughs and fallen leaves.

Harsh and frozen is the earth;
Distant, summer's flowers and mirth;
Gleams alone in thickets damp
The daffodilly's yellow lamp.

One by one the pilgrims go
By the pathway, sad and slow;
Each one thinketh in his heart
How he doth his daily part;

Sorroweth for the sin that kills,
Mourneth o'er the will that wills
Evil 'gainst the high and good
Hero of the holy rood;

Weepeth for a wandering world,
Out of light to darkness hurled;
Prayeth that all feet may come
To the Everlasting Home;

Museth on a brother's pain,
Planneth for another's gain;
Giveth dole to sick and poor,
Out of great or little store;

Traineth self to stand aside,
With denial satisfied;
Smiling on another's bliss,
Adding to his happiness;

Thankful for an ampler share
Than he knows of pain or care.
Counting each a step of light
Reaching to a fairer height.

Pilgrims, we will travel there,
Through the biting wintry air,
On the narrow Lenten road,
Leading o'er the hills to God.

As we wend, it groweth sweet,
And unwearied are our feet
When at last the bloomy spring
Comes to end our travailing.

May we, each one, keep this tryst
With the ever-blessed Christ,

Who will in one fateful day
Meet us on a lonelier way.

ANGELS EVERYWHERE

There flit a myriad angels
About this earth below;
And in and out our thresholds
Their footsteps come and go,
While in our very blindness
Their forms we do not know.

They sing to us in music,
They smile on us in dreams —
They talk to us in echoes
The worldly spirit deems
But chirruping of wood-birds
And chattering of streams.

They make light in our corners,
They purify our air;
They take our hands unconscious,
And guide us unaware.
The presence of their ministry
Is sweetly everywhere.

They sit up in the nursery,
And kiss the babes to sleep.
Across the holy hearth-place
They join their hands, to keep
From blotting out the home-shine
The tears that sad hearts weep.

They lurk about the sick-room,
And trace upon the wall
Quaint legends for still musings
When twilight shadows fall —
The dim world drifting past us,
A thing not worth recall.

Then sit they by the bedside
And hold our passive hands,
And talk to us of strange things
That health scarce understands^
Till home-like to the soul grow
Uncomprehended lands.

They sketch the shadow-groups
And the pictures 'tween the bars,
And point with finger pure
To the tranquil Vast of stars,
While breathing holy peace
On the daylight's petty jars.

They kneel beside the children
Who say their evening prayer,
And flit beside the mother
Who passeth down the stair,
With peace writ on her forehead
Across the print of care.

And when the door is shut,
And the hurried day is gone,
They stand beside the father
Whose labouring is done,
And pay him down the blessings
The children's prayers have won.

LILIES AND ROSES

See these two lilies, growing in the shade —
How like our Mother and the angel by her!
This one, half-folded like the stainless maid;
And that, with wings outspread and heart of fire.

See these two rosebuds, crept within their pale —
Not dazzling-white, nor stately, nor so tall,
Yet pure and tender, owning to be frail,
And love and perfume in their hearts withal.

We may not be the lilies, you and I,
God's chosen blossoms for the fields, above;
But we may be the roses, creeping nigh,
Gaining a nook by dint of longing love.

IN THE DAWN

My soul upon the verge of night
Awakened face to face with God,
By that uncertain tender light

That gleams before the sun's abroad;
And roused from sleep as by a call,
It read a riddle in that hour: —
While singing birds were silent all,
And closed was every blooming flower.

Full many a noon-tide left behind,
I've spent upon the search for this,
That now hath dropped upon my mind
As sweetly as a mother's kiss.
But things that are not seen for light,
Will shine by their own light instead:
So waits the little star for night.
And saintly aureole on the dead.

Had flowers their rosy wings unfurled,
Warm-painted on the azure air;
Had sunshine glamoured all the world,
And birds been singing everywhere,
For song and shine I had not caught
The voice that solved my mystery.
Nor gained this glory to my thought
Which one pale moment brought to me.

Then never, never, weep again
And mourn the sun shine hath gone by,
While faintly through thy window pane
New day may glimmer soberly.
For tracks are seen at paly dawn.
Fresh footprints by the angels made:
And Heaven's full majesty hath shone
On pilgrims travelling in the shade.

GRANDMOTHER'S SONG

The grand-dame sits at the cottage-door
Dreaming, singing, sighing;
The children play on the cottage floor
And watch her needles flying.
And catch the words that fall from her lips
In rambling rhyme and story,
While spring the lights in the harbour ships
And fades the sunset glory.

Many a song of war and pain
Singeth the aged mother —

The strife for love, the strife for gain,
Of men with one another;
Of dauntless sword and fiery fort
Unconquer'd 'mid the burning —
Of ships that gaily sailed from port
And ne'er were seen returning!

And many a song of joy and peace
She crooneth softly after:
Of wounds that heal and tears that cease
And happy fireside laughter;
Of patience long and pardon sweet
And faith of love undying.
The children whisper low at her feet,
"Say, why is granny crying?"

They look in each other's wond'ring eyes
And turn away to ponder.
Out in the burning western skies
Lieth the great world yonder!
And each young soul has chosen here
A verse of the grand-dame's story
To sing through many a coming year,
Of patience, might, or glory.

The agèd mother sleeps at last.
Hushed is the children's prattle:
For one has sailed before the mast,
And one has gone to the battle,
And one in the cottage sitteth long
To keep the hearth-light burning,
And hopeth well and prayeth strong
For wanderers home returning.

O feeble voice that crooneth low,
While babes are round thee playing.
Of human pain and human woe
And Christ's dear love repaying,
What power is thine of song and sigh
To set God's music ringing,
To strike the key-note loud and high
That chimes with angels' singing!

How many a soul that toils amain,
Because the toil is glorious,
And fights with sin and fights with pain
And still comes forth victorious,
Can see in dreams of long ago,

On life's dim threshold yonder.
The agèd mother crooning low,
The babes who list and ponder I

SHAMROCKS

I wear a shamrock in my heart
Three in one, one in three —
Truth and love and faith,
Tears and pain and death:
O sweet my shamrock is to me!

Lay me in my hollow bed,
Grow the shamrocks over me.
Three in one, one in three,
Faith and hope and charity,
Peace and rest and silence be
With me where you lay my head
O dear the shamrocks are to me!

SONG

The silent bird is hid in the boughs,
The scythe is hid in the corn,
The lazy oxen wink and drowse,
The grateful sheep are shorn.
Redder and redder burns the rose,
The lily was ne'er so pale,
Stiller and stiller the river flows
Along the path to the vale.

A little door is hid in the boughs,
A face is hiding within;
When birds are silent and oxen drowse,
Why should a maiden spin?
Slower and slower turns the wheel.
The face turns red and pale,
Brighter and brighter the looks that steal.
Along the path to the vale.

IRENÉ

The monarch Day has flung his crown of gold,
And fiery mantle, down into the river.
And sighing said, "Alas! I have grown old,
I cannot reign for ever and for ever.

"Come hither, Night, my daughter, pure and free,
And let me crown thee with my dying splendour:
Stars for the meek; no passion-tints for thee,
But pensive jewels, radiant, pale, and tender."

Irené hears, and marks the fair young queen.
With dewy tears, and starry brow o'ershaded,
Ascend her skyey throne with silent mien,
And bend towards Earth the mourning. Earth the faded.

Irené hears, for every spirit breath
That flits abroad is by Irene hearkened,
And, reverent, she has knelt as mute as death
Beside the window since her chamber darkened.

The troubled winds are plaining in her ear.
Sure sympathy from lone Irene seeking;
She lifts her face in still suspense to hear
The burden that such smothered sobs are speaking.

A tangled ivy-wreath anear her steals,
And strokes her hair with sad and loving gesture,
The tapestry half wraps her as she kneels,
And swaying stirs her shoulders' cloudy vesture.

The moonlight comes and rims her oval cheek,
Pale gems about her sombre tresses weaving.
And lays upon her brow a silver streak.
And throws beneath her eyes a shade of grieving.

The moonlight comes and floods all through the room.
And pearls the pane, and paints the shadows deeper;
Irene lulls to rest her thought of gloom,
And draws a radiant curtain o'er the sleeper.

A presence now is quickening in the air,
A stately step is through the moonbeams gliding,
A pearly hand is on the maiden's hair,
A gentle voice comes forth with love and chiding.

"My mournful child, why art thou biding lone,
With hush and darkness, weird and spirit-haunted,
While down below, in many a witching tone,

The praises of my beautiful are chanted?

"Thy maidens wait with satin and with gem,
Thy father seeks thee in the Presence Chamber,
For thou must wear the jewelled diadem.
The robe of purple and the veil of amber.

"They wait to hail thee queen of fairest isles,
A golden crown upon thy rich locks placing,
I pine to lead thee to thy throne with smiles,
And see thy form the regal banquet gracing."

The maiden turns, Irene trembling white
With lacing tendril fingers greets her mother:
"Oh! bid me not come forth from hence to-night,
Thou'lt place thy crown upon my little brother.

"I have no wish for satin, nor for gem,
I have no errand to the Presence Chamber,
My brow would ache to wear the diadem:
My limbs shall wear nor purple robe nor amber.

"Inheritance have I in other Land:
I have attained my ripeness to possess it;
The messenger hath becked me with his hand,
His word is law, I may not dare transgress it.

"I've seen the Spirit World its portals ope,
I've felt its breeze about my temples blowing,
I've seen the lustre of the Sun of Hope —
I hardly stayed my eager steps from going.

"Kiss me, sweet mother! do not weep nor frown:
This parting is not sorrow, nor bereavement;
Thy sighs are flowers to weave a fadeless crown, —
Thy tears are diamonds scattered on God's pavement.

"I hear a message borne upon the wind,
The patient Angel guards are kindly waiting.
Oh! may I go, and leave no cloud behind,
No storm within thy tender heart creating!

"My fading eyes no more can see thy face,
Yet strain me to thy bosom, sweetest mother;
Upon the throne a baby form they'll place.
And set the crown upon my little brother.

"Oh, mother! bid me wear the wreath of palm,

And clothe my spirit in the robe of whiteness;
My soul is drifting in a lake of calm,
My sight is blinded by the growing brightness."

MOTHER AND SON

Hungry, and tired, and worn,
Just the age of my Willie;
Dirty, and tattered, and torn —
Ah, well, I am growing silly!
What does it matter to me
If a beggar boy be weary? —
I am craving hopelessly
For the face of my own, own dearie.

Come in, poor boy, and sit down.
Where are thy father and mother?
Dead! and thou'st walked from town.
Begging from one and another;
Hoping for work and bread.
With feet all blistered and bleeding:
And so thy mother is dead,
Thy troubles no longer heeding!

She is not thinking of thee,
Happy herself in heaven —
Just so coldly from me
He went, my boy of eleven.
Spite of my cries and tears,
Spite of my grief and madness.
All through these cruel years
Silent is he in his gladness.

What? — in their glory there
Thou think'st that they still may love us?
We are not shut out from their care
By the bright blue sky above us?
God bless thee, boy, for thy faith,
God bless thee for thy pity;
To make me at peace with death
Thou hast walked a long way from the city!

See, hidden away in a drawer,
Here is my darling's clothing;
When he could wear it no more,
I put it aside in loathing.

Yet oft in a tender dream,
But half in my woe believing,
I have wept o'er each fold and seam
In a frenzy of loving and grieving.

But thou shalt wear them now;
Thou shalt travel and weep no longer,
And the smile on thy youthful brow
Shall make me better and stronger;
And, looking down on me,
Mayhap, thy mother in heaven
Will turn, for dear sake of thee.
And love him, my boy of eleven!

AMONG THE BOUGHS

High on a gnarled and mossy forest bough,
Dreaming, I hang between the earth and sky,
The golden moon through leafy mystery
Gazing aslant at me with glowing brow.
And since all living creatures slumber now,
O nightingale, save only thou and I,
Tell me the secret of thine ecstasy.
That none may know save only I and thou.

Alas, all vainly doth my heart entreat;
Thy magic pipe unfolds but to the moon
What wonders thee in faery worlds befell:
To her is sung thy midnight-music sweet,
And ere she wearies of thy mellow tune,
She hath thy secret, and will guard it well!

JUNE

O lovely June, sweet giver of young roses,
A wild and tearful spring has vexed us long,
Chiding the opening bud and wood-bird's song,
But now her wilful reign unwilling closes!
O fill thy lap with flowers, and come to us,
Leaning thy face, with soft carnations glowing.
Out of the fragrant boughs, from southward blowing,
And let us see thee in thy" beauty thus!
Now we will track thee through mysterious alleys
Of long-enchanted forest greenly dim —

The mossy quire of moonstruck nightingales;
Or, waked by faint notes when the darkness pales,
Fleeing along the ocean's kindling rim,
We'll follow thee across the rose-wreathed valleys!

HOPE DEFERRED

A dreariness came o'er me
Once, on a dim spring day;
The summer on before me
Seemed far and far away.

Full dark had reigned the winter,
With cloud, and mist, and gloom;
My spirit longed to enter
Into the fields of bloom.

The tempest's wild repining
Made sorrow in my soul;
I craved the cheerful shining
When heavy clouds unroll.

I saw a gleam on heather
Stray through a rifted cloud;
The masses swept together.
The winds spoke fierce and loud.

The mist upon the mountain
Dropped down in hopeless rain;
Fell in a bitter fountain
Over the grieving plain.

THEN AND NOW

In that sweet olden time of May,
When all the chestnuts were in bloom,
O'ershadowed was with tender gloom
The silence of the long brown way.

Beyond the shadowed moss-grown wall
The laughing meadows lay in light,
Half golden-green, half drifts of white.
Around the feet of oak-trees tall.

A pallid moon from out the blue
Was hanging, leaned above the trees.
Far-gazing over distant seas.
Yearning to lovelier worlds she knew.

Most sweetly tuned the hidden thrush;
The corn-crake from the hollow near
Kept saying loudly, "Summer's here!"
Across the dream-like noon-tide hush.

Then your glad spirit spoke to mine,
"The summer's here, and love is ours;
So crown, O love, my soul with flowers,
And straitly bind my life to thine!"

With roses thrice I bound thy hands,
Low laughing in the shadows warm;
God keep our love from blight and harm,
We wander now in separate lands!

Deep shadows gloom the long brown way,
The thrush sings low from out the green;
The summer is less sweet, I ween,
Than it was in that olden May!

MAY DITTY

Cuckoo! cuckoo! for love and mirth
My heart is gay;
I have no wish, no wish on earth,
Sweet, sweet, 'tis May!

The swallows on my roof awake
With twittering notes,
In chorus full, as though they'd break
Their little throats.

Cuckoo! cuckoo! I hear it sing
From out the grove,
And all the hills are echoing
The voice of love.

Sweet dreams from off my eyelids go,
I live again;
I hear the rosebuds talking low
About the rain.

I hear the lambs upon the lea,
The throstle's brood;
The flowing music of the sea,
The breathing wood.

I hear the panting of the brook,
I hear the sigh
O' the lily that the water shook
When hurrying by.

Rise, little head, all golden-ringed,
Lent me by God!
Wake, little spirit, angel-winged.
And flit abroad!

Wee baby in thy tiny bed
Come, crow again!
I'll gather thee that jewel red
Set in our pane!

I'll deck thee all in snowy state.
Monarch of spring!
With crimson roses from the gate
I'll crown thee king.

The birds shall pipe and tell our sport
To all things gay.
And we will hold a merry court
This first of May!

PERDITA

I dipped my hand in the sea,
Wantonly —
The sun shone red o'er castle and cave;
Dreaming, I rocked on the sleepy wave; —
I drew a pearl from the sea,
Wonderingly.

There in my hand it lay;
Who could say
How from the depths of the ocean calm
It rose, and slid itself into my palm?
I smiled at finding there
Pearl so fair.

I kissed the beautiful thing,
Marvelling.
Poor till now, I had grown to be
The wealthiest maiden on land or sea.
A priceless gem was mine,
Pure, divine!

I hid the pearl in my breast,
Fearful lest
The wind should steal, or the wave repent
Largess made in mere merriment,
And snatch it back again
Into the main.

But careless grown, ah me!
Wantonly
I held between two fingers fine
My gem above the sparkling brine,
Only to see it gleam
Across the stream.

I felt the treasure slide
Under the tide;
I saw its mild and delicate ray
Glittering upward, fade away.
Ah then my tears did flow,
Long ago!

I weep, and weep, and weep,
Into the deep;
Sad am I that I could not hold
A treasure richer than virgin gold,
That Fate so sweetly gave
Out of the wave.

I dip my hand in the sea,
Longingly;
But never more will that jewel white
Shed on my soul its tender light;
My pearl lies buried deep
Where mermaids sleep.

MY TREASURE

I have a treasure. What is it, say,

O lady fair, O lady fair?
Is it a mirror to shine all day,
Or pearls to braid my brown, brown hair?

A diamond buckle to clasp my shoon?
A satin robe — like the glistening crest
Of the lake that ripples under the moon —
Zoned with rubies beneath my breast?

Is it a castle with broad, fair lands?
A magic purse of caged red gold.
Whose swelling meshes within my hands
Exhaustless store of riches hold?

Is it some wondrous beauty-charm,
To steep my lips in brilliant dyes.
To mantle my neck in tresses warm,
And tint my cheek and light my eyes?

Is it a crown and a throne of state,
I And a wand to wave o'er subjects leal,
With mailèd guards at my palace-gate,
And a royal will to say and seal?

I tell thee, no: it is none of these,
O lady fair, O lady fair!
But a little babe upon my knees,
To toss and pull my brown, brown hair.

A FLEDGLING

A bird was sheltered in my breast
That sang both night and day,
And had I toil or had I rest
That birdie sang alway.

I sleeked its feathers 'gainst my heart,
And laughed to hear it sing;
The wind kissed not in any part
A sweeter, blither thing.

It piped upon the hedge-row green.
It sang up in the blue,
At morn it bathed in sunlight sheen.
At eve it sipped the dew.

On one green bough it perched at night
And trilled through all my dreams,
And wakened me at peep of light
To see the first dawn-gleams.

It cooed so soft of moonlit eves
I dared not let it sing,
But covered it with red rose-leaves,
Its head beneath its wing.

I swore that we should never part,
And then I let it fly. —
No music have I in my heart,
No more until I die.

KILFENORA

A dream lives in the purple of thy hills,
A spirit haunteth thee for evermore,
Kilfenora!
Out of that dream she cometh when she wills,
That spirit, and walketh on thy wild sea-shore,
Kilfenora!

A small white sea-bird on thy wave below
Sits long and broods and rocks upon thy flood,
Kilfenora!
The storm within my heart how can she know,
Yet she doth know and all hath understood,
Kilfenora!

The violet and the song-bird have their nests
In thy green lap, and they are sweet in thee,
Kilfenora!
But sweeter far the dream within my breast,
Scenting my thoughts and singing piteously,
Kilfenora!

O sweeter far the dream that lived and died,
A summer's life and then a winter's grave,
Kilfenora!
In thy fair valley and on thy strong tide.
That gave and took, and taking all, yet gave,
Kilfenora!

A REBUKE

Why are you so sad? (sing the birds, the little birds)
All the sky is blue,
We are in our branches, yondep are the herds,
And the sun is on the dew;
Everything is merry, sing the happy little birds,
Everything but you!

Fire is on the hearthstone, the ship is on the wave,
Pretty eggs are in the nest.
Yonder sits a mother smiling at a grave,
With a baby at her breast;
And Christ was on the earth, and the sinner He forgave
Is with Him in His rest.

We shall droop our wings (pipes the throstle on the tree)
When everything is done:
Time unfurleth yours, that you soar eternally
In the regions of the sun.
When our day is over (sings the blackbird in the lea)
Yours is but begun!

Then why are you so sad? (warble all the little birds)
While the sky is blue,
Brooding over phantoms and vexing about words
That never can be true,
Everything is merry (trill the happy, happy birds),
Everything but you!

NIGHT AND MORNING DREAMS

I wake from dreams of the night,
And the stars aloft are coldly gleaming;
My dream was dark and strange with woe:
Oh foolish heart! dost thou not know
The dreams that are dreamed 'neath the stars' pale light
Are nought but idle dreaming!

I wake from dreams of the morn,
And the sun on high is shining fairly,
The lark in the blue is singing far,
Seeking in vain for the midnight star,
And the buds of the roses newly born
Blush through their dew-drops pearly.

My dream hath fled from the light.

But my heart is warm where its face was shining;
Oh happy heart! thou knowest well
What the morning dream doth sure foretell,
Thine onward path will be glad and bright.
Arise! and forswear repining!

THE HEART OF RACHEL

I am the mother of seven,
Yet never a child have I;
At least, I have none beside one.
None this side of the sky.

The first was born in sunshine,
A blue-eyed cherub boy:
God meant him to be an angel —
I made of him a toy.

So God in wrath recalled him.
And gave him wings above.
Then first I learnt in my grieving
The might of a mother's love.

The second, a fairy darling,
Was wondrous bright to see.
I made of her an idol —
Her life was snatched from me.

I groaned with a heart unchastened,
I wept away my sight;
The eyes of my third sweet baby
Oped never on the light.

The fourth had a wild, high temper —
I gave his pride the rein:
God struck him with His lightning,
And left me lorn again.

The next was a proud, high maiden,
None yet so fair had been.
I chafed at her humble birthright —
She should have reigned a queen.

The jewels paled on her forehead,

The roses in her hair —
The shroud was the richest raiment
Her dainty limbs would wear!

And then a son was given me,
Who burned with sacred fire,
The gaining of souls for Heaven
His passion's one desire.

He had no pride of bearing,
Nor beauty in mine eyes;
He turned his glad face from me,
And travelled toward the skies.

But a daughter came with comfort,
And tarried near me long;
God's music carolled round her,
Her life was all a song.

Her spirit flashed with genius,
She sang to the souls of men;
My nature's hoard of worship
Was poured out on her then.

I loved her with haughty loving:
She sank 'mid shadows drear;
She fled to her heaven, and left me
Alone and weeping here.

PERPETUAL LIGHT

O soul, be not so sore afraid
To see the coming night;
Go forth to meet it undismayed,
For — after the darkness, Light!

The clouds lean down, the shadows close,
Dear eyes fade out of sight;
But under the black earth hides the rose
And — after the darkness, Light!

The stars are quenched, the path is lost,
Feet fail to move aright;
But, harvests wait beneath the frost,
And — after the darkness, Light!

Heart-broken, blind, O strive no more.
With shadows cease to fight;
See! dawn is breaking on yon shore,
And — after the darkness. Light!

The prostrate will accepts of death,
The soul submits to night.
Rise in thy splendour, Sun of Faith —
After the darkness, Light.

SAINT BRIGID

'Mid dewy pastures girdled with blue air,
Where ruddy kine the limpid waters drink,
Through violet-purpled woods of green Kildare,
'Neath rainbow skies, by tinkling rivulet's brink,
O Brigid, young, thy tender, snow-white feet
In days of old on breezy morns and eves
Wandered through labyrinths of sun and shade.
Thy face so innocent-sweet
Shining with love that neither joys nor grieves
Save as the angels, meek and holy maid!

With white fire in thy hand that burned no man
But cleansed and warmed where'er its ray might fall.
Nor ever wasted low, or needed fan,
Thou walk'dst at eve among the oak-trees tall.
There thou didst chant thy vespers while each star
Grew brighter listening through the leafy screen.
Then ceased the song-bird all his love-notes soft.
His music near or far.
Hushing his passion 'mid the sombre green
To let thy peaceful whispers float aloft.

And still from heavenly choirs thou steal'st by night
To tell sweet Aves in the woods unseen,
To tend the shrine-lamps with thy flambeau white
And set thy tender footprints in the green.
Thus sing our birds with holy note and pure
As though the loves of angels were their theme;
Thus burn to throbbing flame our sacred fires
With heats that still endure;
Thence hath our daffodil its golden gleam,
From thy dear mindfulness that never tires!

POVERTY

I had a dream of Poverty by night,
And saw the holy palmer wending by
With pensive mien and radiant. upturned eye,
Drinking the tender moon's approving light.

I saw her take the hills and climb the height.
While broad below the city murmured nigh,
Spangling the dusk with lamps of revelry
That made the mellow planets pale to sight.

Yet kept my love her face toward the stars
Till broke the dawn against the mountain ridge
And angels met her on the misty way;

Then heaven looked forth on her through golden bars.
Then gleamed her feet along a rosy bridge,
Then passed she noiseless into eternal day.

AFTER THE STORM

Mary most pure, walking in highest heaven
Among the blossoms of the starry meadows,
And looking down into our earthly shadows,
Heard a sad soul that asked to be forgiven.

Pausing, she listened to the piteous story;
Then said she, " I will have for my handmaiden
This weary soul with sorrow overladen.
And I will robe her in eternal glory."

Behold the eager angels hastening
Where Death and Satan hover o'er their prey,
While Sin and Poverty are standing by.
For each his own, and none will dare deny

To Death and Poverty the worn-out clay: —
"Wake, happy Soul, and spread thy trembling wing!

NORAH' S LILIES

"Norah, little Norah! whither art thou hieing?"

Keep the sad voices of the winds calling eerily.
"Aha! for the water, for the blue shining water!"
Rings out the answer from her glad heart cheerily.

Still snatching wildly at her curly brown locks streaming —
"Linger on the heath awhile and revel with us merrily!"
"Hie! for the lilies, for the white floating lilies!"
Leaping from the clinging of their light hands airily.

"Tarry, little maiden, the waxen cups come drifting "—
Dragging in terror at her light flowing drapery.
"O they are for Mary! and the dawn-star is fading;
Morn is breaking o'er the hills, pallid and vapoury."

"Tarry, little Norah! thou'lt drown unless thou tarry!
We will blow the flowers, so thou mayst grasp them easily! "
"They must be on the altar at Mary's feet ere sunrise," —
Stretching o'er the margin of the lake curling breezily.

Rest thee, little maiden, thou art drifting 'mid the lilies,
Down among the lilies with thy dead eyes closed dreamily,
Clasping to thy bosom all the snowy waxen blossoms,
While upon thy pallid face the sun smiles beamily.

"Norah, little Norah! it is sunrise on the mountains!"
Wail the sad voices of the winds calling drearily;
"Mary wears the lilies in her diadem in Heaven,"
Weird Echo answers, through the mist falling eerily.

GONE FROM EARTH

Stars are shining over the sea —
Where is she? O where is she?
Swept away on the winter wind,
Leaving the rain and the mist behind.

Hyacinths white were by her head,
She lay so still on the ghostly bed —
Ghostly bed with its pillars grim,
Cover of snow and hangings dim.

Stars are shining over the sea,
Where is she? O where is she?
Hurried away on the winter's breath —
The world is blank and full of death.

Where is she, with her spirit-eyes?
The lamps are lit in the dusky skies:
I see them glimmer afar, afar, —
I journey toward the evening star.

Beautiful gate of a distant heaven!
Ever towards thee my soul is driven.
Voices are crying, "Come, O come!"
I struggle to reach the spirit-home.

FAILURE

The Lord, Who fashioned my hands for working,
Set me a task, and it is not done;
I tried and tried since the early morning.
And now to westward sinketh the sun!

Noble the task that was kindly given
To one so little and weak as I —
Somehow my strength could never grasp it,
Never, as days and years went by.

Others around me, cheerfully toiling.
Showed me their work as they passed away;
Filled were their hands to overflowing.
Proud were their hearts, and glad and gay.

Laden with harvest spoils they entered
In at the golden gate of their rest;
Laid their sheaves at the feet of the Master,
Found their places among the blest.

Happy be they who strove to help me,
Failing ever in spite of their aid!
Fain would their love have borne me onward,
But I was unready and sore afraid.

Now I know my task will never be finished,
And when the Master calleth my name
The Voice will find me still at my labour,
Weeping beside it in weary shame.

With empty hands I shall rise to meet Him,
And, when He looks for the fruits of years,
Nothing have I to lay before Him
But broken efforts and bitter tears.

Yet when He calls I fain would hasten —
Mine eyes are dim and their light is gone;
And I am as weary as though I carried
A burthen of beautiful work well done.

I will fold my empty hands on my bosom,
Meekly thus in the shape of His Cross;
And the Lord Who made them frail and feeble
Maybe will pity their strife and loss.

SISTER MARY OF THE LOVE OF GOD.

This is the convent where they tend the sick,
Comfort the dying, make the ailing strong;
Covered, you see, with ivy, very thick;
Haunt of the birds, alive with bloom and song.

The happy sick are smiling in their beds,
The happy sisters flitting to and fro;
Ah, blessings on the wise and gentle heads
That planned this place a hundred years ago!

To build the walls a woman crossed the sea,
Travelled with tender feet a weary road.
I'll tell you now the little history
Of Sister Mary of the Love of God.

A lovely maiden of a high estate,
She danced away her days in careless glee;
A bird beside her window came and sate,
And piped and sang, "The Lord has need of thee!"

Deep in the night, when everything was still,
The restless dance, the music's merry clang,
That bird would perch upon the window sill:
"The Lord hath need of thee" it piped and sang.

She rose and fled her chamber in affright,
And roused with eager call the minstrel gray:
"The birds are singing strange things in the night;
Tune me, O minstrel, something blythe and gay!"

The minstrel struck his harp with ready power;
The laughing echoes wakened merrily:
The lady turned as white as lily-flower —

The music trilled, "The Lord has need of thee!"

Her guests came round her, and her ball-room blazed,
While lively footsteps on the floor did beat:
The lady led the dance with looks amazed —
"The Lord doth need thee!" said the dancers' feet.

The feast was spread, and flowed the rarest wine
In golden goblets clinking round the board:
The flashing cups from hand to hand did shine,
And rang and chimed "Go, give thee to the Lord!"

Within her chamber long the lady sate,
Then raised her downcast face, all pale and sweet:
"There is a beggar lying at the gate —
Go, bring him in, that I may wash his feet."

They looked upon her robes of satin sheen,
They looked upon her eyes so strange and glad:
They whispered, "She is not as she hath been;"
Her damsels wept, "Our lady hath gone mad!"

But in the night she stole away alone.
Then sang the minstrels many a mournful rhyme,
Till some forgot her as one never known.
And others said, "She hath some heavy crime."

Ah me, it is a hundred years ago! —
This ivy on the walls is thick, you see;
The world would laugh if I should tell it so
Of Sister Mary's little history.

Another dances in her shoes to-day;
One wears that gem of hers, another this;
But she is happy and the poor are gay,
The sick are smiling and the dead in bliss!

SUN AND RAIN

My life awoke in a dawn of tears,
Dull rain kept falling all through the years;
Harsh winds would threaten and never hush.
I pined for skies that might glow and flush;
For buds that blossom and beams that shine,
Gladdening the world, yet never mine.
My life was dark, I pined for such —

I asked too much, I asked too much'

I murmured, "The falling, soaking rain,
Doth feed and fatten the hidden grain;
Doth cover the field with fruitful gold.
Doth hang the mist in the purple wold;
Doth swell the river and fill the stream,
While weaving the rainbow's coloured dream.
And tears are good, thou hast need of such —
Ask not too much, ask not too much."

I said, "There is need of sunshine too,
Or what will the tender fruitage do,
When growing erect and slight and tall?
If ever the showers will fall and fall,
What smile will ripe the sickening grain,
Beneath the smileless hueless rain?
I ask for sun, I have need of such —
I ask too much, I ask too much.

The rain dropped on as the rain will drop.
When the sun laughs out and bids it stop.
It flashed its jewels here and there —
They trembled aslant adown the air,
Glittered from grassy and mossy nooks,
And among the pebbles anigh the brooks.
A draught of sun! I had need of such;
I drink, I drink, and it glads me much.

The air is wondrous pure and still.
The morning gleameth on moor and rill;
The rain-clouds drift, and drift away;
I whisper, "My soul, my soul, 'tis May!"
Look to the sky whence late the showers,
Look down and behold their gift— the flowers.
What boon. is this? Dost thou merit such?
Art praying much? Art praying much?

My soul hath terror to make reply.
It throbbeth dumbly beneath the sky,
"My work is little, my prayer is weak!"
Such are the words my soul would speak.
For all this boon I have nought to give;
My life is God's, and I can but live —
Live, not hoping to merit such.
But fearing much, but fearing much.

My life is glad in its early May,

My morn expecteth a sunny day —
A noon all glowing, an eve of rest.
With warm gleams lingering within the west;
And starlight winning, ere late they die,
Its holier sway athwart the sky.
My hope is new, and my dreams are such,
I ask too much, I ask too much.

And I ask it not, pray but to be
Something that praiseth and gladdeth Thee —
An incense-wreath, a breath of song,
A flower white-hearted to lay along
The golden path that the Angels trace,
Repassing and passing before Thy face.
Some small pure thing (and I would be such),
That feareth nothing and loveth much.

OUR LILY

A bed of lilies basking in the sun,
Their snow-white petals blushing ever faintly, —
Their cups are brimming with the golden light,
That hovers round them with a radiance saintly;

A young laburnum drooping from the wall,
Upon the path its golden blossoms trailing.
Just thrilling to the echo, sweetly soft,
Of winds in distant forests sadly wailing;

Framed with the leaves my baby-Lilian stands —
The lilies love their little human sister, —
And shed their light around her sunny curls.
And, swaying, touch her cheek as though they kissed her.

She stands, with wide blue eyes and lips apart,
A bright carnation in her fingers crushing.
Lost in an infant reverie of joy
To see the kindling West and mountains flushing.

My little golden-headed lily-bud,
Say, canst thou penetrate those realms of splendour
That hide but mystery all vague and dim
For eyes less spirit-like and souls less tender?

And do thy snow-white kindred whisp'ring tell
Rare secrets of those far-off glorious regions,

And does thy sinless gaze e'en now behold
The gleaming pinions of their angel legions?

Look at me, pet! and not so wistful-wise —
We cannot spare thee, even to the angels:
We need thy smile, thy tiny tripping feet,
Thy small voice chanting little sweet evangels.

I've seen that yearning look in other eyes
That now are closed, and in the green earth sleeping;
But thine are of another shape and tint —
Thou earnest to bring us laughter and not weeping.

Ho! for a race — and then thou tell again
The words I taught thee, funny little lisper!
My birdie, come! and never mind the sky —
Thou must not listen while the lilies whisper.

A DREAM'S LESSON

I laid me down, a-murmuring and weeping —
O Christ! assuage the pain,
And send some dream of comfort in my sleeping
To ease my wearied brain!

I slept; and there I saw an angel folding
His wings beside my bed:
A thorny garland in his fingers holding
Above my shrinking head,

Saying: "Christ sends to thee the richest blessing
His might hath got to give,
That thou, with humble gratitude possessing,
Mayst, thankful, wear and live."

So pressed he down his wreath of cruel seeming
Upon my bleeding brow;
And, oh! such anguish quivered through my dreaming:
I feel its burning now!

"I thank thee, who this bitterness hath given!"
I cried, and with the prayer
The anguish passed, and healing balm from Heaven
Came through the gentle air —

And kissed the wounds, and wiped away the bleeding.
And wooed away the pain:
And filled my heart with tenderness exceeding,
And soothed my weary brain.

The cruel sting of thorns no longer knowing,
But wreathed with dewy leaves,
I breathed the scent of flowers all newly growing
On showery summer eves.

My happiness aroused me from my sleeping —
My fateful dream was o'er;
With wondering peace I hushed away my weeping —
I waked, and wept no more.

AVE MARIA!

Come, run with me, O stalwart youth and maiden!
And run with me, O children young and fleet! —
And even ye with years so heavy-laden,
Now struggle yet to use your failing feet!

Come, crowding forth from all the lanes and alleys.
Come, hurrying out from all the fields and woods,
And make your paths in all the pathless valleys.
And leave your tracks on all the trackless floods!

For unto earth has come a mighty wonder.
And sweeter words are spoken now by God,
Than when of old He spake to us in thunder,
And scourged the faithless nations with His rod.

Oh come and see the lily He has planted —
Eve's fairer daughter, blooming in the land;
And make again the prayers that He has granted,
And ask the world's redemption at His hand!

For lo! the stars in Heaven's serenest story
Are grouped to crown this womanhood sublime,
And lo! the sun has woven of his glory
A robe to be her raiment for all time!

Oh come, and see a spotless Virgin kneeling,
Oh come, and hear an angel, at her side,
The earliest tidings of our joy revealing —
The herald of the glorious Christmastide.

Come here, for this is Mary and no other,
And she will nurse the Lord upon her knee;
And Jesus will bequeath her as a mother
To us upon the Cross of Calvary.

Then let us run, and greet her with the angel;
Ave Maria! give to us thy Son!
O'er all the earth ring out the loud evangel —
The gates of hell are closed, and Heaven is won!

IN THE GARDEN

Lord, the place is dark with night,
The olive trees are dim to sight;
Scarcely can I see Thee, prone,
Face to earth, outcast, alone.

I have followed Thee with fear,
Followed Thee, and found Thee — here.
Tet me cry, and let me pray.
Take the cup of pain away!

Hear me pray and hear me cry
Words of Thine own agony:
Thou the Lord, and God of all;
I, so poor, so weak, so small.

Yet no coward, and if Thou
Urgest this, give courage now!
Calm the shudder at my heart,
Bid my rebel will depart.

Let the measure be filled up,
Filled and drained the bitter cup —
Drained, O living God, for Thee,
Who hast made this mystery!

AN OUTCAST'S PRAYER

Dear Lord! admit me to Thy sanctuary —
The dawn shines through Thy door,
And O the night has been so wild and weary!
Say, shall I wander more?

I will not ask to look upon Thy glory,
Lord, if Thou let me in;
Nor weary Thee with any piteous story —
Thou know'st the ways of sin.

Make signal to me, Lord, with pitying gesture,
Thy peace to me were dear;
The heavy rain of tears is on my vesture,
My heart is cold with fear.

Fugitive from Thine enemy's enslavement,
I seek Thy bondage sweet.
My grateful kisses, rained upon Thy pavement,
Shall glow beneath Thy feet

My steps have grieved the highways with their bleeding
While hastening to Thy side.
Thy glory would be saddened by my pleading
If I were still denied.

Look on the face of Thy fair Mother, Mary,
Ne'er shadowed by a sin,
Whilst angels ope Thy longed-for sanctuary
To take Thy suppliant in.

O let me in to shelter everlasting!
I weep against Thy door.
For hope of rest my weary soul is wasting —
Say, shall I wander more?

A PRAYER

Give me, O Lord, a heart of grace,
A voice of joy, a shining face,
That I may show where'er I turn
Thy love within my soul doth burn!

Though life be sweet and joy be dear,
Be in my mind a quiet fear;
A patient love of pain and care.
An enmity to dark despair;

A tenderness for all that stray,
With strength to help them on the way;
A cheerfulness, a heavenly mirth,

Brightening my steps along the earth;

A calm expectancy of death.
Who bloweth out our human breath;
Who one day cometh in Thy name
And putteth out our mortal flame!

Press Thou Thy thorns upon my head,
For I would bleed as Thou hast bled;
'Tis meet that I should wounded be
By that which sorely wounded Thee!

I ask, and shrink, yet shrink, and ask:
I know Thou wilt not set a task
Too hard for hands that Thou hast made,
Too hard for hands that Thou canst aid.

So let me dwell all peacefully.
Content to live, content to die,
Rejoicing now, rejoicing then,
Rejoicing evermore. Amen!

Rosa Mulholland – A Concise Bibliography

Dunmara (1864) (Writing as Ruth Murray)
Hester's History (2 volumes 1869)
The Wicked Woods of Toobereevil (2 volumes 1872)
Eldergowan, or Twelve Months of My Life & Other Tales (1874)
Five Little Farmers (1876)
Puck and Blossom: A Fairy Tale (c1879)
Four Little Mischiefs (1883)
The Wild Birds of Killeevy (1883)
Hetty Gray, or Nobody's Bairn (1883)
The Walking Trees & Other Tales (1885)
The Late Miss Hollingford (1886)
Marcella Grace, an Irish Novel (1886)
Vagrant Verses (1886)
A Fair Emigrant (1888)
Giannetta: A Girl's Story of Herself (1889)
The Little Flower Seekers (188-?)
The Haunted Organist of Hurly Burly & Other Stories (1891)
The Mystery of Hall-in-the-Wood (1893)
Marigold & Other Stories (1894)
Banshee Castle (1895)
Nanno, a Daughter of the State (1899)
Onora (1900)

Terry, or She Ought to Have Been a Boy (1902)
Cynthia's Bonnet Shop (1900)
The Squire's Grand-Daughters (1903)
A Girl's Ideal (1905)
The Tragedy of Chris: The Story of a Dublin Flower-Girl (1902)
Life of Sir John Gilbert (1905)
Our Boycotting, a Miniature Comedy (1907)
The Story of Ellen (1907)
Our Sister Maisie (1907)
Cousin Sara (1908)
The Return of Mary O'Murrough (1908)
Spirit and Dust (1908)
Cousin Sara, a Story of Arts and Crafts (1909)
Father Tim (1910)
The O'Shaughnessy Girls (1911)
Fair Noreen, the Story of a Girl of Character (1912)
Twin Sisters, an Irish Tale (1913)
The Cranberry Claimants (1913)
Old School Friends: A Tale of Modern Life (1914))
The Daughter in Possession: The Story of a Great Temptation (1915)
Narcissa's Ring (1916)
O'Loughlin of Clare (1916)
Price and Saviour

As Editor

The Life and Adventures of Robinson Crusoe (1886)
Fifty-Two Stories of Girl-Life at Home and Abroad (1894)

www.ingramcontent.com/pod-product-compliance
Lightning Source LLC
Chambersburg PA
CBHW060038050426
42448CB00012B/3068